The Vacation Activity Book

Jane Bull

DK Publishing

LONDON, NEW YORK, MUNICH,
MELBOURNE, and DELHI

DESIGN • Jane Bull
EDITOR • Penelope Arlon
PHOTOGRAPHY • Andy Crawford
DESIGN ASSISTANT • Gemma Fletcher

PUBLISHING MANAGER • Sue Leonard
PRODUCTION • Georgina Hayworth
DTP DESIGNER • Ben Hung
JACKET EDITOR • Mariza O'Keeffe

For Charlotte, Billy, and James

First American Edition, 2007

Published in the United States by
DK Publishing
375 Hudson Street, New York, New York 10014

07 08 09 10 10 9 8 7 6 5 4 3 2 1

A catalog record for this book
is available from the Library of Congress.

ISBN 978-0-7566-2942-7

Color reproduction by
GRB Editrice S.r.l., Verona, Italy
Printed and bound by Toppan, China

Discover more at
www.dk.com

A book packed full of vacation fun...

Your vacation activity kit 4-5

Fold-away game mats 6-7

Sticky play tin 8-9

Sticky furry felts 10-11

Food on the move 12-13

Travel tubs 14-15

Crunchy vacation postcards 16-17

all packed up...

Keeping cool 18-19

Stencil your style 20-21

Design your stencil 22-23

Ted's on tour 24-25

Wish you were here! 26-27

My vacation book 28-29

How to shape a book 30-31

...and ready to go!

Nature walk 32-33

Nature activities 34-35

Beach art 36-37

Pebble heads 38-39

Your souvenir shop 40-41

How to make souvenirs 42-43

Things to do 44-45

Are we there yet? 46-47

Index 48

Your Vacation activity kit

Pack up your pens! Be prepared for some creative fun on your vacation—make your own kit.

Make a kit box

YOU WILL NEED:
A box (a shoe box is ideal), colored paper, thin cardboard, and cord.

Shoe box with lid

Make four holes.

Add handles

Thread the cord through the holes.

Tie knots on all four ends, making sure the knots are big enough.

...Pack up your materials in the sections.

The larger pads of paper will fit on the top.

What's in the kit?

Here are a few essentials you could pack for lots of creative fun.

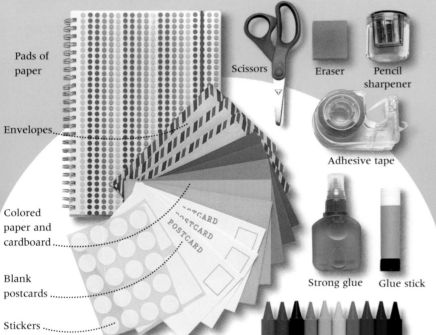

Pads of paper

Scissors

Eraser

Pencil sharpener

Envelopes

Adhesive tape

Colored paper and cardboard

POSTCARD
POSTCARD
POSTCARD

Blank postcards

Strong glue

Glue stick

Stickers

Pencil

Wax crayons

Felt-tip pens

Paints

Colored pencils

Ruler

Mini paints and pencils can save space.

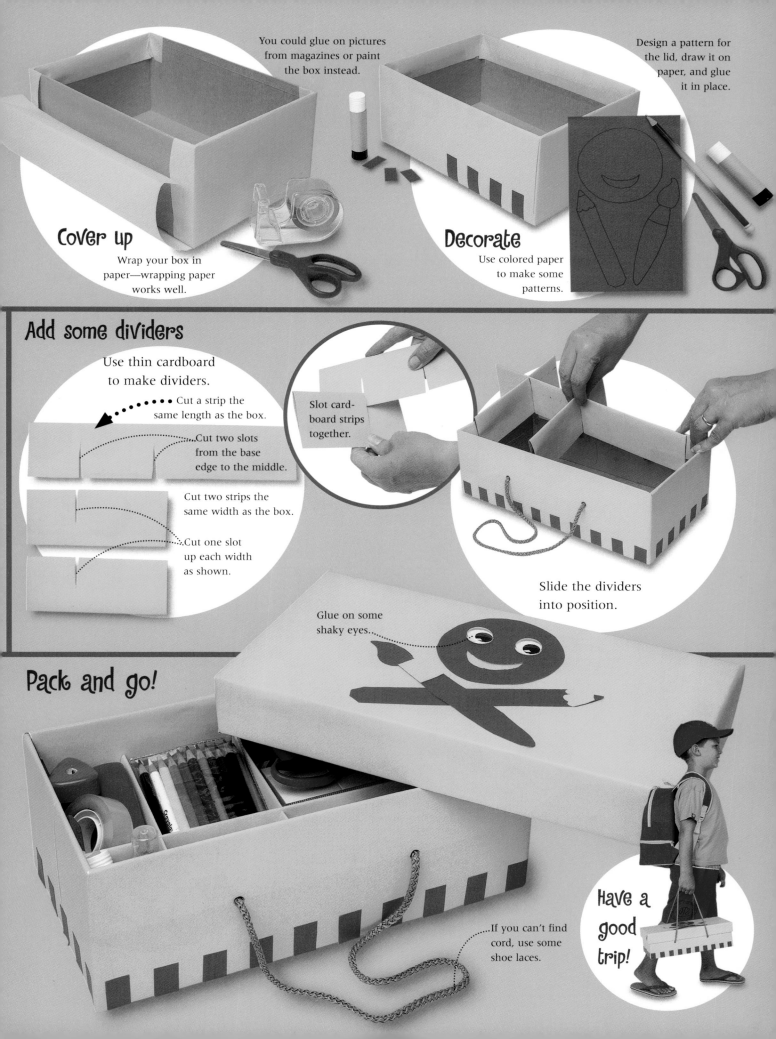

Cover up

You could glue on pictures from magazines or paint the box instead.

Wrap your box in paper—wrapping paper works well.

Decorate

Design a pattern for the lid, draw it on paper, and glue it in place.

Use colored paper to make some patterns.

Add some dividers

Use thin cardboard to make dividers.

Cut a strip the same length as the box.

Cut two slots from the base edge to the middle.

Cut two strips the same width as the box.

Cut one slot up each width as shown.

Slot cardboard strips together.

Slide the dividers into position.

Pack and go!

Glue on some shaky eyes.

If you can't find cord, use some shoe laces.

Have a good trip!

Fold-away game mats

Anywhere and everywhere—make a game mat that folds up neatly in your box.

Your mat will need to fold up small enough to fit in your box.

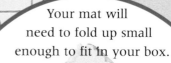

......You can use anything as counters, even your snacks!

Fold-up game board

Find a piece of white material to make a fold-away board. White cotton is good, since it will fold up nice and small.

Cut out a piece of white cotton, 12 in by 12 in (30 cm by 30 cm).

With a ruler mark every 1 in (2.5 cm) across and down.

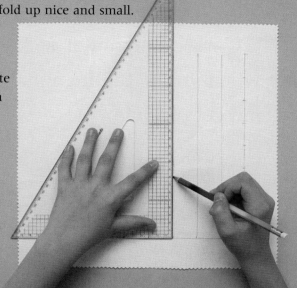

Draw in the lines, making sure you have 8 boxes by 8 boxes in the center of the cotton.

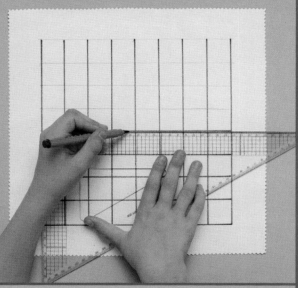

Color in every other square. No colored square should be next to another colored square.

Snakes and ladders

Your board can be adapted to snakes and ladders, checkers, chess, or any other board game. Just cut out felt shapes to suit your game.

Ready to play?

Make sure you learn the rules of the game you choose to play, then unfold the mat and play away!

Sticky play tin

Another portable game box—this time full of sticky games that will stay in place when you're on the move. Pack up your tin, get sticky, and get playing!

Metal tin

Why use a tin container?

Magnets will stick to the lid of a metal box, such as an old cookie tin. You can make pictures and write messages and they won't slide around.

Foam or cardboard shapes with magnets glued to the back.

Fridge magnet letters and numbers

What's in the box?

Letter and number magnets

Write a message, play a word game, do some math, or make funny faces.

it's all boxed up

keep your odds and ends together by finding small boxes that will fit neatly into your tin. They'll keep everything neat and tidy.

Fold-away game mat

Here's the perfect place to store your game mat.

Felt shapes

Furry felt shapes are great for making pictures. Turn over the page for some shape ideas.

Inside the lid

Glue a piece of felt to the inside of the lid. You can then make pictures out of felt pieces.

Lap top

Open your tin when you're on the move or on the beach!

Sticky furry felts

Felt sticks really well to felt so you can make felt pictures without them sliding away—perfect for moving vehicles.

Dab glue in each corner.

Your felt shapes will stick to this surface.

1 Inside the tin lid

Cut a piece of felt to fit inside your tin lid and glue in place.

2 Glue it flat

Now you have a nonslip surface to place your shapes on.

Cut circles, squares, flowers, leaves, and any other shapes you can think of.

3 Cut out shapes

Now all you need to do is cut out lots and lots of felt shapes.

Keep the shapes in a box and store it in your tin.

Now make a picture

Cut out a tangram

Use the template opposite to cut out your tangram shapes.

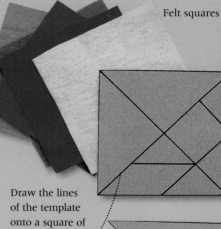

Felt squares

Draw the lines of the template onto a square of thin cardboard.

Cut along all of the lines.

Now put each shape on a square of felt and draw around it.

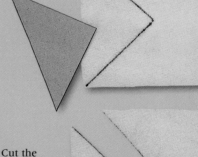

Cut the shape out.

Repeat with all the shapes.

Tangrams

What is a Tangram?

It's a Chinese puzzle made by cutting a square into six triangles, one square, and one rhomboid. These shapes can all be rearranged to make hundreds of different pictures.

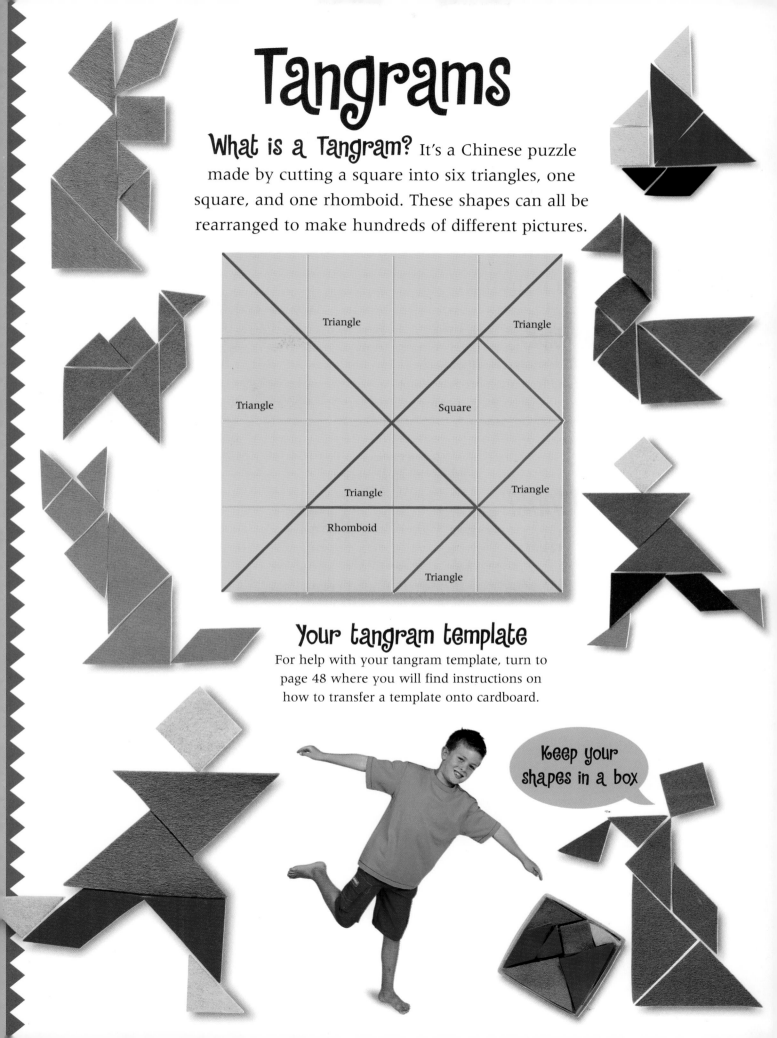

Triangle

Triangle

Triangle

Square

Triangle

Triangle

Rhomboid

Triangle

Your tangram template

For help with your tangram template, turn to page 48 where you will find instructions on how to transfer a template onto cardboard.

Keep your shapes in a box

Food on the move...

Pack up some fast food for a long trip. Bite-sized snacks like grapes, nuts, and vegetable sticks all boxed up in airtight containers are perfect when you're hungry.

Food travel tips

- Don't take too much sugary or salty food.
- Fresh vegetables and fruit are more refreshing.
- Feeling car sick? Try ginger—it's good for your digestion and may settle your stomach.

We're on our way!! Crumbs!

GINGERSNAP
COOKIES

FRESH,
CRISP
APPLE

HEALTHY
OAT
BARS

NUTS AND
SEEDS

JUICY
GRAPES

CHERRY
TOMATOES
AND
RADISHES

Bite-sized

Small pieces of food are sometimes all you need to keep you going on a long trip. After all, if you're cooped-up in a car you won't need lots of extra energy.

YUMMY
CHEESE
DIPS

PEAS AND
BEANS FOR
DIPPING

PRETZELS
AND CORN
SNACKS

CARROT AND
CUCUMBER
STICKS

Gingersnaps

 Makes 16 cookies

Into a bowl goes:

1 cup (100 g) self-rising flour

²/₃ cup (40 g) granulated sugar

1 tsp ground ginger

1 tsp baking soda

4 tablespoons
(50 g) butter

Set the oven to
375°F, 190°C

Put all the
ingredients into
a mixing bowl.

Rub it together using
your fingertips.

2 tablespoons
corn syrup or
honey

Use your hands
to squeeze the
mixture into a ball.

1 Rub it together then add the syrup   2 Make a big ball

Travel tubs

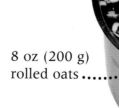

Air-tight containers will keep
your food fresh throughout a
trip and will stop anything from
spilling out.

Rough track oat bars

 Makes 24 bars

Into a saucepan goes:

²/₃ cup (50 g) soft brown sugar

2 tablespoons corn syrup
or honey

6 tablespoons
(75 g) butter

Set the oven to
375°F, 190°C

Add the oats.

Put the
sugar, syrup,
and butter into
a saucepan.

Heat the pan and
mix together as
the butter melts.

Ask an adult
to help with
the hot pan.

8 oz (200 g)
rolled oats

Keep stirring
until the oats
are mixed in.

TURN OFF THE HEAT!

1 Melt it down   2 Add the oats

Divide the ball into 16 pieces.

Roll each piece into a ball.

Nonstick cookie sheet

Place the balls on the cookie sheet and press them down with a fork.

Ask an adult to help with the oven.

Bake for 10–15 minutes
You may need to cook them in two batches. When they are done let them cool down on a rack.

3 Make into small balls

4 Squash them

5 Bake them

Load up the beans, we're off!

Pour into a nonstick baking pan—about 8 x 12 in (20 x 30 cm).

Press the mixture down and out to the edges.

Use the back of the spoon.

Cut into bars while still slightly warm.

When they have cooled, remove the oat bars.

Ask an adult to help with the oven.

Bake for 20 minutes.

3 Pour into pan

4 Press it down

5 Bake and cut

Crunchy Vacation postcards

Cookie postcard
Bake some yummy shortbread cookies, have fun painting your vacation scenes on them, and give them to a friend.

16

Making the cookies

Makes 8–10 cookies

1 1/2 cups (150 g) flour

Set the oven to 325°F, 170°C

8 tablespoons (100 g) butter

1 cup (50 g) sugar

1 Rub it together

Put all the ingredients in the bowl and rub them together with your fingers until the mixture is crumbly.

Sprinkle flour on the surface to stop it from sticking.

2 Roll it out

Squeeze the mixture into a ball. Sprinkle flour on the table and roll out the dough to 1/4 in (5 mm) thick.

3 Cut into rectangles

Use a knife to cut the dough into rectangles. Collect up the leftovers and roll them out again.

4 Place on the tray

Grease a cookie sheet then carefully transfer the dough onto it. The cookies are now ready for the oven.

5 Bake then cool down

Bake in the oven for 10–15 minutes.

Ask an adult to help with the oven.

Paint your cookies

When the cookies have cooled down they are ready for painting. Remember to keep your brush clean.

Let the cookies cool on a wire rack.

Paint directly onto the cookie.

Pour drops of food coloring into a palette.

Wash the brush with water each time you change color.

Wish you were here!

Pour some fruit juice into an empty cup.

Reuse small dessert cups.

Push a ice pop stick through some cardboard.

The cardboard keeps the stick upright.

Push the stick to the bottom of the cup.

Put the cup into the freezer.

Try making lots of different flavors.

Drink on a stick

Squeeze and freeze! Buy some fruit juice or squeeze your own, then freeze it into refreshing ice pops.

Be patient, it will take at least six hours to freeze. If you can, leave it overnight.

Take the cardboard off and pull it out of the cup—a delicious ice pop.

Keeping cool

"Phew! It's a hot day, I could use something delicious to cool me down." Look no further—these icy creations are perfect for a hot day or a long trip.

Blueberries

Black and green grapes

Strawberries

Red currants

Lemonade

Plastic spoon

Plastic cup

Put the fruit and a spoon in a plastic cup and fill with lemonade.

Cut some cardboard to fit the top of the cup.

Push the spoon through a hole in the cardboard.

Carefully put it into the freezer overnight until it's solid.

Frozen fizzy fruit cups

Use fresh fruit and lemonade for these fizzy fruit ices.

Fresh fruit

REMEMBER Keep the cardboard on the cup until you are ready to eat the ice.

Keep the cup so when the ice pop melts you can eat the fruit with the spoon.

Cool for long trips

Put a bottle of water or juice in the freezer overnight. Take it out just before your trip and it will keep cool for most of the day.

Make mini fruit cups using small dessert cups and tiny spoons.

Buy an atomizer from a drugstore and fill it with fresh water.

Refresh your face.

Frozen fruit drinks

19

stencil your style

Personalize your stuff.

Choose a motif, cut out a
stencil, and print, print,
print—it's as easy as that!

Print matching sets

Make large and small stencils.

Vacation kit box

Stencil everything!
Once you have decided on your design, you can stencil lots and lots of things from notebooks and boxes to bags and caps.

Backpack

Notebook

Hat

..Use a smaller version of your design.

Keep it simple
The trick to stenciling is to keep the designs very simple. Create your own logo—it could be a vacation theme or your favorite activity.

Prepare your shirt

A clean, white shirt will work best because the paint shows up well, but a pale color will work too.

The material needs to be completely flat to get the best print. Put a piece of cardboard inside the shirt to stop it from ruffling up.

Use a stiff piece of cardboard that will fit inside your shirt.

Insert the cardboard right up to the neckline.

REMEMBER—whatever you cut away will be where the ink goes through.

Use thin cardboard for the stencil; cereal-box cardboard works well.

Design your stencil
Keep the image simple

Use the piece of stencil cardboard to draw on your design. Bold simple shapes work best—they are easier to cut out and paint through. Stencils look better if you have more than one cutout in the design. This way you can use more colors too.

If you can't get fabric paints, you could use acrylic paints instead.

Paint your design

Fabric paints are the best to use—they work like ordinary paints but will not wash out when you clean your clothes. Follow the makers' instructions on the jars.

Use the paints straight from the jars.

Tape your ste in place at the top and botto

Don't put too much paint on the brush.

Paintbrush with hard bristles

Dab on the paint

Fold the shirt around the cardboard and tape in place.

Cut out another piece of cardboard and use it as a template to mark out the background of the design. Put tape around the edges of the cardboard, then remove it.

Make a background

Paint a color within the tape.

Leave it to dry.

Add the color

Ask an adult to help you cut out the design.

Little and large
Make smaller stencils for caps or notebooks.

Paint all the colors before you remove the stencil.

Remove the stencil and allow the paint to dry.

Peel back the stencil

Iron over the pattern to fix the paint—follow the instructions on the paint jar.

Ask an adult
to help with ironing.

Ready to go!

Ted's on tour

Your favorite toys can take a trip too. Set them up with their own vacation kit.

I'm Ted look after me

Paper parasol

Ted at the beach

Search through your stuff for things that are Ted's size.

Wash cloth

This tiny toy camera was on a keyring.

Toy boat

Ted's own magazine

Small plastic container for orange juice

Passport Tedland

Smile please!

Here is a great way for you to record your trips. Take a photo of a favorite toy enjoying what you are enjoying.

Ted's passport

Ted needs a passport to go on vacation. Fill in his personal details and add some pictures to show what he's been up to.

Ted's ID cardboard

ID cover

ID inside page

1 Take two pieces of cardboard. Fold them in half and glue the white cardboard inside the cover.

2 Take Ted to have his photo taken.

3 Design a symbol for the front cover and glue it place.

Use colored paper for the design.

TED'S ACTIVITIES

OFFICIAL

NAME .... **Ted** ....
PLACE MADE .... **wooltown** ....
DATE KNITTED .... **10/10/06** ....
HEIGHT .... **12 in. (30. cm)** ....
SPECIAL FEATURES .... **one slipped stitch** ....

4 Fill in Ted's details and use stickers or draw where he has been.

Out and about

A day at the beach

A trip to the city

Ted's album

Wherever you are, take a picture of Ted enjoying the scenery, having a meal, relaxing on the beach, or on the road. It's a different way of recording your trip too.

Yum yum

This is the best!

You could show them...
your favorite meal, the beach you have been to, your friends, or your family on the road. Perhaps there are some unusual plants or animals around.

At the camp

Ours is the RED one!

Wish you were here!

I'm having a great time!

Make your friends envious by sending them a postcard you've drawn yourself.

Postcards

Paints or pens

Pen or pencil

To Grandma
The house
Up the street
Back home

Stamp goes here

To make your card

Take a blank postcard from your kit, draw a picture in pen or pencil, then color it in using paints or crayons.

27

A book for the beach

1

My vacation

V

Bon Voyage

Z

A book for a road trip

A book for a museum trip

My Vacation

Pack a suitcase book with all your vacation memories.

Suitcase diary

This suitcase diary is perfect to store your vacation memories in. You can fill it with photos, tickets, and any other souvenirs.

Glue one handle to each piece of cardboard.

Cover the cardboard with colored paper.

To make the covers, cut out two pieces of cardboard from cereal boxes.

Draw two handles on a piece of paper.

Glue the paper to pieces of cardboard and cut out.

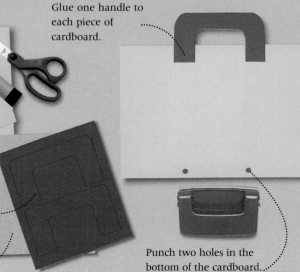

Punch two holes in the bottom of the cardboard.

Tickets and tags

Save everything! Wherever you go collect your tickets, tags, and momentos to paste in your book.

Snapshots

Take photos of your visits and glue them in. You could create a photo story of your day.

This is where I went...

...and here

Collect leaflets from places you have visited and cut out the pictures.

Collect some postcards from your travels.

This was the view from the plane!

Cut out pieces of colored paper the same size as the cover.

Cut triangles of paper to paste to the corners of the book.

Punch two holes in the bottom of all the pieces of colored paper. Slip the paper between the two covers.

Thread string or ribbon through the holes and tie a bow.

Your suitcase is ready to pack!

Decorate your shell book with glitter and goggle eyes.

Stick in favorite shells and pebbles...

My beach vacation

Save some sand in a bag and stick it in.

The sand tickled my toes...
Try writing a poem about the beach or sea. Is the sea shallow or deep? Is it calm or are there waves? Is the beach sandy or pebbly?

Sparkly ribbon

How to shape a book

A book doesn't have to be book-shaped; it can be any shape you like! Think about what kind of vacation you will have and design a shape that suits the trip. Use the instructions on page 28 to make the book, but change the shape.

Drawing pictures
Save some of your home-made postcards to paste in your book.

Draw pictures of yourself and your family and put them in the window of your car.

My road trip

Let's go!
How are you traveling on your vacation? Why not design a car book, plane book, or boat book?

Copy the shape of your own car.

Book-o-saurus

"We went to a dinosaur museum and we saw a…" Perhaps you are going to make a special trip on your vacation that will give you the shape of your book.

Decorate the cover as a dinosaur face.

Pick up a souvenir pencil… …to fill in all the facts!

My visit to the dinosaurs

Include your ticket, a map, and leaflets from your day.

Today I saw the…

Write a description of what you see, sketch pictures, and collect some facts and figures along the way.

biggest ....
smallest ....
longest ....
most ferocious ....

....

....

Cut out pictures from papers and magazines.

Draw pictures of things you have seen on your trip.

Dear diary

Why not try writing a diary of your whole vacation? Fill it in at the end of each day. Tell your diary what you have done that day, what you ate, and any exciting events.

Fill in a new page each day.

Nature walk

off for a stroll?

Collect as you go! You'll be
amazed what you can
do with a good nature
collection. Keep an eye
out for leaves, seeds, and
a bird's feather or two.

Superbug collection

Create your very own collection of creepy crawlies. Butterflies with flapping wings and tiny beetles with nutshell wing cases, all held together on clay bodies.

Nature bugs

Lay out the things you've collected. Are you inspired by any of the shapes?

How to make a nutty bug

Add cherry-stalk legs.

Roll out a clay head and body.

Give it a nutshell back and wings.

The Green King head-dress

How to make a leafy crown.

Tape the ends together.

Tape lots of leaves to the cardboard.

Cut out a piece of cardboard that will fit around your head, with extra length to attach the ends.

Wise owl eyes

How to make a leafy mask.

Nutshells

Smaller leaves make a border.

Draw a mask shape onto a piece of thin cardboard, making sure that the eye holes are the same width apart as your eyes.

Acorn beak

Cut out the mask.

The stake will allow you to hold the mask up to your face.

Tape a plant stake to the back of the mask.

Use strong glue to stick leaves to the mask shape.

Always remember to take a bag with you on a nature walk to put the collection in.

A fancy frame

Make a natural frame to show off a painting or photograph.

Cut a frame out of cardboard that has thick enough edges to glue on your nature collection.

Ask an adult to help cut out the frame.

Use strong glue to attach all kinds of leaves, seeds, feathers, twigs, pinecones, and anything else you might find.

Follow the country code
Do respect the countryside.
Do stay on the footpaths.
Do close gates after you.
Don't pick wild flowers.
Do try to collect things that have fallen from trees and are on the ground.
Don't go out on your own;
ALWAYS TAKE AN ADULT.

Painted pebbles
Fishy stones and patterned pebbles make great presents.

Beach art
A visit to the beach gives you plenty of material to play with. Try instant art or gather some beachy bits and make art at home.

Standing stones
Instant art on the beach.

Pebble people
There are lots of pebble faces on the beach—it's up to you to find us.

Fishtails
Put stones together to make different shapes.

Goggle-eyed

Pebble pals

Sandman
Make faces in the sand and let the sea wash them away.

Patterns and scenes

Vrooom!

You'll need lots of us!

Pebbles make great art. Make patterns and faces on the beach, or take them home to play games with and create gifts for friends.

Search for shapes that work best for faces.

Pebble heads

Practice pebble faces on the beach then take them home and glue the stones together.

Add goggle eyes...

Use a strong glue to stick them together.

Beachcombing

As you play on the beach, fill up a bucket with odds and ends that catch your eye. Take it home and start creating.

Hello sandy face!

Not all pebbles are round; some are odd shapes. This one looks just like a nose. Look for them and make happy, sandy faces.

Painting pebbles

Acrylic paint is thick and waterproof so it is perfect for painting pebbles. Paint it right onto the pebble—you may need two coats of paint for a perfect finish.

Wash your brush out between colors.

Apply the first coat and wait for it to dry.

To make the paint less see-through, add some white paint.

Mini cakes

Make a miniature picnic. Take small stones and paint them to look like delicious creamy cupcakes.

Rings and things

Make your pebbles and shells into precious jewelry. You will find ring bases and claws for pendants in local craft stores. Use strong glue to attach them.

Rings

Brooch back

Shells for ears and a painted face

Pendant claws

Spread out the claw's prongs and use strong glue to press it to the pebble or shell.

Add string to make a necklace.

3-D scenes in a box

Bag them up and give them away.

Your souvenir shop

It's fun to buy mementos on vacation, but it's even more fun to make your own to keep or give away.

Snow globes

Mini pet Dinosaur in a jar

Plaster pictures

3-D picture

Make a scene that reminds you of your vacation.

Woodland walk

Collect pinecones, twigs, and nut-shells to set in plaster.

Set the scene in a wooden cheese box.

Wherever you go and whatever adventures you have, make sure you remember them by turning things you have collected along the way into art. Then let friends know how good your vacation was by giving your art away as presents.

Happy vacation

Reuse glass jars to make a magical scene.

Snowstorms

Mini pets

Give a home to a tiny plastic animal in a jar.

A piece of cloth held on with a rubber band

Transform plastic models in glitter and glycerine.

Plaster plaques

Plaster of Paris is really easy to use but it dries quickly, so work fast! You can buy it in local craft stores. Use any old plastic containers you find to make perfect presents or keepsakes.

MIX THE PLASTER
For a small container:
2 tablespoons plaster
4 tablespoons water

A plastic bottle base makes a good shape.

Plaster of Paris

You could use any plastic trays—like these food trays.

Add some water…

…and stir.

The mixture should be like whipped cream—not runny. Add more water or plaster until it's right.

1 Stir in the water

Snowstorms

Mix up a snowstorm to remind you of your vacation. To make it sparkle you need a very clean glass jar with a screw-top lid. Use a strong glue—not a glue that will dissolve in water.

Screw-top glass jar

Glycerine

Glycerine can be bought in drug-stores. It is thick and helps the glitter move in the water.

Plastic or ceramic toy

Glitter

Strong glue

Glue the toy to the inside of the lid.

Leave the glue to set.

Fill a jar just over halfway up with water.

3-D Scenes

These 3-D pictures are made out of layers of paper, with a wedge stuck between each layer to give the 3-D effect. Collect the lightweight, wooden boxes that come with things such as cheese—they can be transformed into some great art.

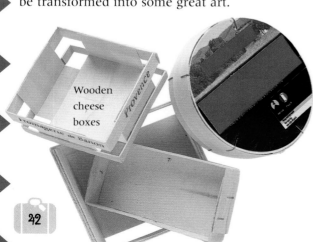

Wooden cheese boxes

Draw around the box to make a template.

Cut out the template and use it to cut out lots of pieces of colored paper the same size.

Scoop the mixture into the tray.

Give the tray a few sharp taps to make the plaster settle.

Press the objects into the plaster.

Collect odds and ends, such as shells and pebbles, from a beach.

Leave it to dry for 30 minutes.

Hold the tray upside down over your hand.

Let the plaque drop out.

2 Fill the mold   3 Make your design   4 Let it set   5 Turn it out

Pour in 2 tablespoons of glycerine.

Stir it up.

Add a teaspoon of glitter.

Stir it again.

Fill up the jar with more water.

Lower the lid onto the jar.

Don't worry if the water spills over.

Wipe the jar and check for leaks.

Add more glue around the lid to seal it.

NOW SHAKE IT!

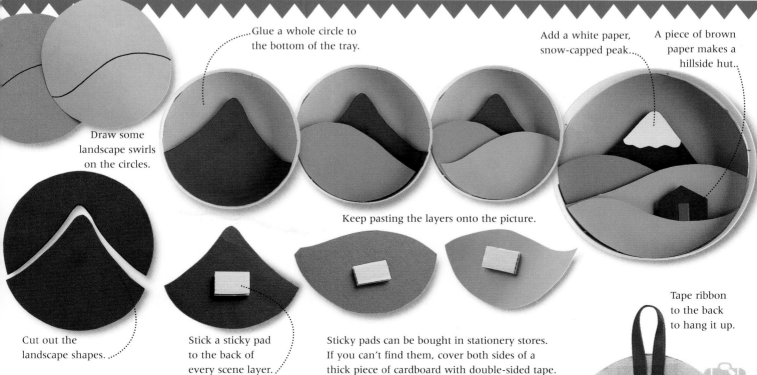

Glue a whole circle to the bottom of the tray.

Add a white paper, snow-capped peak.

A piece of brown paper makes a hillside hut.

Draw some landscape swirls on the circles.

Keep pasting the layers onto the picture.

Cut out the landscape shapes.

Stick a sticky pad to the back of every scene layer.

Sticky pads can be bought in stationery stores. If you can't find them, cover both sides of a thick piece of cardboard with double-sided tape.

Tape ribbon to the back to hang it up.

43

Things to do

VIP for a day!

Bite into your cupcake. If you get the one with the cherry in it, you are a Very Important Person and YOU get to choose what to do for the ‸ day.

What will you choose? Perhaps…

- be treated like royalty for a day?
- you get to sit in the front seat?
- you choose the movie?
- you get to go first—anywhere?
- choose the restaurant?

Take a bite…
I've got it!

4 tablespoons (100 g) butter

1/2 cup (100 g) self-rising flour

1/3 cup (100 g) sugar

2 eggs

1 Mix it up
Put all the ingredients in the bowl and beat un‸ the mixture is ligh‸ and fluffy.

2 One cherr‸
Put some cupcake cases in a muffin pan. Take ONE cherry and place it in ONE of the cases.

3 Cover up
Spoon the mixtur‸ into the cases, making sure you cover the cherry completely.

Set the oven to 375°F, 190°C

4 Bake
Bake in the oven for 10–15 minutes.

Ask an adult
to help with the electric beater and the hot oven

Finish each cupcake with a cherry on the top.

5 Decoration
Mix some confectionary sugar with a few drops of water and spoon it on top of the cupcakes.

22

Draw a monster...

...with your friends. Take a piece of paper and draw a head at the top. Fold the paper down and pass it to the next person, who draws the top of the body. They fold it down, and pass it on as shown. When it's finished, open it up and there is the mystery monster! Remember—don't show anyone what you are drawing.

1
Draw a head.

2
Draw the top of a body...

3
...then the bottom...

4
...and finally the legs.

Open it up.

What a very strange monster!

What shall we do?

Can't decide what to do? Why not let the jar be your guide? Write down different ideas on pieces of paper, fold them up, and put them into a jar or box. Then when you just can't decide what to do, dip in.

- Let's get out the paints.
- Let's go to the movies.
- Let's go on a bike ride.
- Let's play cards.

Let's bake cupcakes

Let's go swimming

Let's go to the zoo

What happened next?

Who knows where the story will begin or end! The great thing about this game is that you all get to listen to a story—but no one knows what will happen next...

Pick someone to start a story and let them make up the story for half a minute. When their time is up, the next person picks up the story where it stopped and continues it for another half-minute. The last person has to end the story.

HERE ARE A FEW STORY IDEAS TO START YOU OFF.

Dad promised us that he knew the way to the beach, but as they climbed higher and higher up the mountain, they had a feeling they were lost...

OR

One fine day a toad and a frog were sunning themselves by a small stream. Suddenly they heard a loud BANG!

OR

It all started when James went to Tom's house to play football...

45

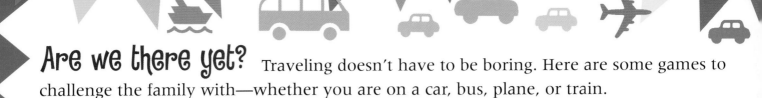

Are we there yet?
Traveling doesn't have to be boring. Here are some games to challenge the family with—whether you are on a car, bus, plane, or train.

Grandma's suitcase

How good is your memory? Test it with "Grandma's suitcase." List the things Grandma has packed to go on her vacation. The things she packs can be a wild as you like, all you have to do is remember them—here's how it goes...

My Grandma went on vacation and in her suitcase she packed:
...a pair of flippers

The next person repeats the above then adds another packed item.

My Grandma went on vacation and in her suitcase she packed:
...a pair of flippers
...and a pet kitten

Keep going until someone gets an item wrong or can't remember one and gives up.

It might end up sounding like this...

My Grandma went on vacation and in her suitcase she packed:
...a pair of flippers
...a pet kitten
...a set of drums
...a cabbage
...her best sweater
...an umbrella
...and a small frying pan
...and on and on!

Travel bingo

Keep the cards together in a CD case.

How to make your game
Cut out some square pieces of paper the size of a CD case. Draw lines down the cards so there are three boxes across and three boxes down. Now draw a picture in each box—draw things that you might see on a road trip.

How to play travel Bingo
Give each person in the car (except the driver!) a card and tell them to check the picture when they see it outside the car. When you have checked all the boxes shout "BINGO!"

Give each player a pencil so when they match a picture they can check it off their card. To play again, just erase the pencil marks.

Words on plates

Look at a license plate. You'll notice that there are letters on it. When you are on the road, pick a car, look at the license plate, and race each other to make a word out of the letters. The letters must stay in the same order but the word can be as short or long as you like. Watch out, some letter combinations are really difficult!

I spy
I spy with my little eye, something beginning with "s"...
Is it a sign?
Is it a scarecrow?
Is it a street lamp?
I know, it's my sunglasses!
All you have to do is think of something you can see, then tell the family the first letter. The first person to guess the word wins.

Red car, yellow car
Pick a color and count the number of cars you see in that color. The first to reach ten wins!

I see 10 I'm the winner!

Patterns for stencils

Copy these shapes to use as stencils for your prints (pages 20-23). Turn over to page 48 to find out how to transfer the designs onto a piece of cardboard.

Ask an adult to help you cut out the shapes.

Transferring the tangram onto card-board
(from pages 10-11)

Use this method for your stencils as well.

Lay a piece of tracing paper over the shape.

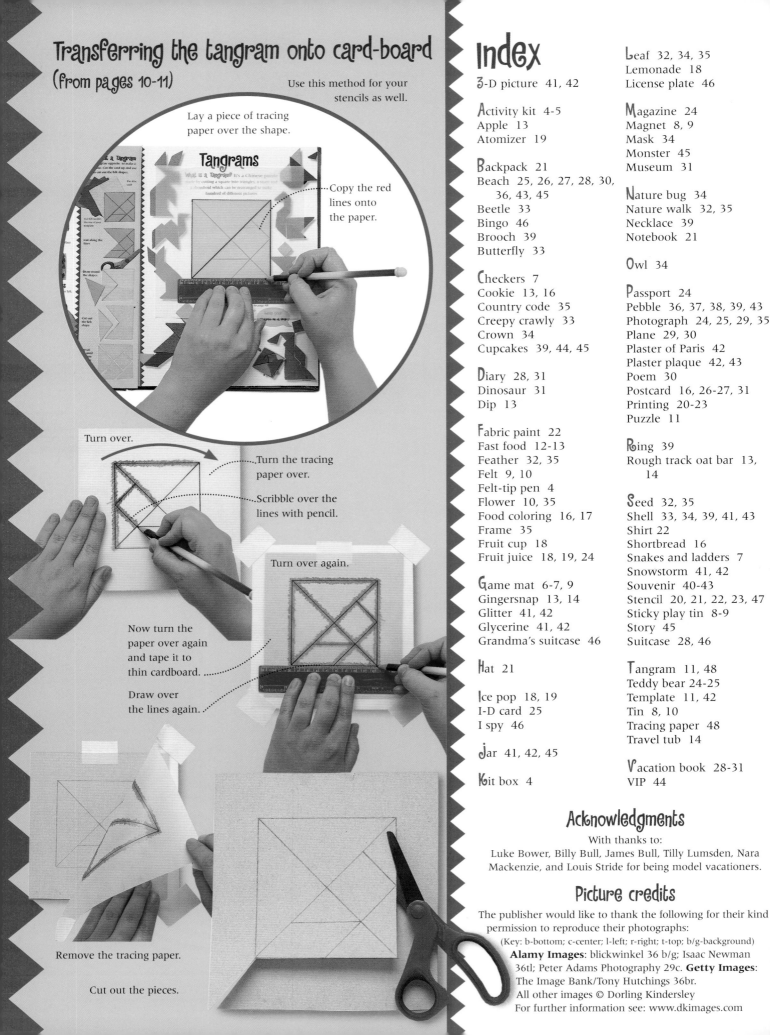

Copy the red lines onto the paper.

Turn over.

Turn the tracing paper over.

Scribble over the lines with pencil.

Turn over again.

Now turn the paper over again and tape it to thin cardboard.

Draw over the lines again.

Remove the tracing paper.

Cut out the pieces.

Index

3-D picture 41, 42

Activity kit 4-5
Apple 13
Atomizer 19

Backpack 21
Beach 25, 26, 27, 28, 30, 36, 43, 45
Beetle 33
Bingo 46
Brooch 39
Butterfly 33

Checkers 7
Cookie 13, 16
Country code 35
Creepy crawly 33
Crown 34
Cupcakes 39, 44, 45

Diary 28, 31
Dinosaur 31
Dip 13

Fabric paint 22
Fast food 12-13
Feather 32, 35
Felt 9, 10
Felt-tip pen 4
Flower 10, 35
Food coloring 16, 17
Frame 35
Fruit cup 18
Fruit juice 18, 19, 24

Game mat 6-7, 9
Gingersnap 13, 14
Glitter 41, 42
Glycerine 41, 42
Grandma's suitcase 46

Hat 21

Ice pop 18, 19
I-D card 25
I spy 46

Jar 41, 42, 45

Kit box 4

Leaf 32, 34, 35
Lemonade 18
License plate 46

Magazine 24
Magnet 8, 9
Mask 34
Monster 45
Museum 31

Nature bug 34
Nature walk 32, 35
Necklace 39
Notebook 21

Owl 34

Passport 24
Pebble 36, 37, 38, 39, 43
Photograph 24, 25, 29, 35
Plane 29, 30
Plaster of Paris 42
Plaster plaque 42, 43
Poem 30
Postcard 16, 26-27, 31
Printing 20-23
Puzzle 11

Ring 39
Rough track oat bar 13, 14

Seed 32, 35
Shell 33, 34, 39, 41, 43
Shirt 22
Shortbread 16
Snakes and ladders 7
Snowstorm 41, 42
Souvenir 40-43
Stencil 20, 21, 22, 23, 47
Sticky play tin 8-9
Story 45
Suitcase 28, 46

Tangram 11, 48
Teddy bear 24-25
Template 11, 42
Tin 8, 10
Tracing paper 48
Travel tub 14

Vacation book 28-31
VIP 44

Acknowledgments
With thanks to:
Luke Bower, Billy Bull, James Bull, Tilly Lumsden, Nara Mackenzie, and Louis Stride for being model vacationers.

Picture credits
The publisher would like to thank the following for their kind permission to reproduce their photographs:
(Key: b-bottom; c-center; l-left; r-right; t-top; b/g-background)
Alamy Images: blickwinkel 36 b/g; Isaac Newman 36tl; Peter Adams Photography 29c. **Getty Images**: The Image Bank/Tony Hutchings 36br.
All other images © Dorling Kindersley
For further information see: www.dkimages.com